SKYSCRAPERS

SKYSCRAPERS

BY BEN SONDER

MetroBooks

MetroBooks

An Imprint of Friedman/Fairfax Publishers

©1999 by Michael Friedman Publishing Group, Inc.

Library of Congress Cataloging-in-Publication Data

Sonder, Ben
    Skyscrapers / by Ben Sonder.
       p.   cm.
    Includes bibliographical references and index.
    ISBN 1-56799-828-3
    1. Skyscrapers. 2. Architecture, Modern—19th century.
  3. Architecture, Modern—20th century. I. Title.
    NA6230.S63 1999
    720'.483—dc21   99-16236
                                  CIP

Editor: Emily Zelner
Art Director: Jeff Batzli
Designer: Joseph Rutt
Photography Editor: Sarah Storey
Production Manager: Camille Lee

Color separations by Fine Arts Repro House Co., Ltd.
Printed in Hong Kong by Midas Printing Limited

1 3 5 7 9 10 8 6 4 2

For bulk purchases and special sales, please contact:
Friedman/Fairfax Publishers
Attention: Sales Department
15 West 26th Street
New York, NY 10010
212/685-6610 FAX 212/685-1307

Visit our website:
www.metrobooks.com

CONTENTS

INTRODUCTION

Architect Bradford Lee Gilbert was terrorizing Manhattan's business community. His new building for the wealthy silk-maker John Noble Stearns would be known as the Tower, a narrow slab of iron, terra-cotta, and cement, not much more than 39 feet (12m) on its widest side and only 21½ feet (6.6m) at its entrance on lower Broadway. Unfortunately, a score of architects, journalists, engineers, and politicians had New Yorkers up in arms about the new structure. They were sure that its narrowness, as well as its extraordinary height and depth, would make it a public menace.

Finally, an engineer decided to take matters into his own hands. He wrote a letter to owner Stearns about the building's

Opposite: Fiercely dominant, the World Trade Center rises from the southwestern tip of Manhattan, not far from the shores of the Hudson River. Its twin towers are so notoriously distracting that many people do not know the complex is composed of six buildings around a central plaza.

potential instability and then personally delivered a copy to the architect. The letter stated plainly that he thought the tall building was doomed to blow over, endangering lives in downtown Manhattan and damaging other structures around it. Because Gilbert had a permit from the New York Department of Buildings, he went ahead with his audacious project. But on a Sunday before construction was finished, New York was struck by a 70-mile-per-hour (112kph) gale. In downtown Manhattan awnings rattled, and trees in the parks lost a good share of their leaves. Gilbert rushed downtown to check on his skyscraper. It was surrounded by a crowd of onlookers waiting for the big crash. He grabbed a plumb line and began climbing ladders left by the workmen. When he finally approached the top of his building, the wind was so strong that he had to drop to his hands and knees. Then he sank the plumb line along the side of the building. Just as he had predicted, not the slightest vibration was evident. Gilbert's faith in his skyscraper had proved justified.

The miracle of Gilbert's solid, wind-braced tower made the papers and silenced critics. Everyone was astonished that a skyscraper that tall, and especially one that slender, could withstand so much wind. The year was 1889. Gilbert's skyscraper was only ten stories tall.

DEFINING THE SKYSCRAPER

The word *skyscraper* is just as it sounds: a fanciful, rather exaggerated term designed to communicate people's awe and excitement about tall buildings. In reality, its meaning has changed radically in the hundred or so years since it came into our language. In the 1890s a building of ten stories more than qualified as a skyscraper, but today the term is rarely used to describe a building of fewer than fifty stories.

Quaint as the late nineteenth-century take on the word may seem, it must be kept in mind that our own seemingly sophisticated concept of the skyscraper is destined for a speedy extinction. Skyscrapers of 150 stories and more—mostly destined for the Far East, which has become the new frontier of the skyscraper—will soon redefine old standards like the Empire State Building, with its mere 102 stories.

To be deemed a skyscraper, a building must first of all qualify as a high rise. And a high rise is merely any building taller than the height people are willing to walk. Thus, all high rises—and therefore all skyscrapers—require elevators. Another essential quality of the skyscraper is that it is too tall to be supported by its own walls. Unlike the preskyscraper building, which relied on the masonry of its walls to withstand gravity and wind, the skyscraper is supported primarily by a rigid metal skeleton, upon which its walls are hung like curtains. Once the details of building such a structure were mastered, skyscrapers could be constructed quickly, and their popularity increased.

Above: McGraw-Hill Building II, Manhattan. At fifty-one stories high, this structure, built in 1973, has unique vertical steel striping and a 15-meter abstract steel sculpture by Athelstein Spilhaus called Sun Triangle.

Opposite: The sixty-story Nations Bank in uptown Charlotte, North Carolina, is the tallest in the city and has become the most identifiable structure in the skyline. Its unique crown-like roof is visible from almost any point in the uptown section.

Above: Atlanta's Peachtree Center. A view of the Hyatt Regency from beneath the sculpture "Ballet Olympic."

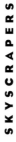
Right: Seen from the freeway at dusk, downtown Los Angeles debunks the city's reputation for wide-open sprawl. Currently, it is undergoing a spell of fervent commercial and cultural development. In 1998, the Japanese American National Museum Pavilion opened. Meanwhile, new commercial tenants are flocking to downtown's oldest buildings in the El Pueblo historic district surrounding Olivera Street.

Left: The Chicago skyline has become an eclectic cluster of high rises. On the left stands the Amoco Tower.

The development of the skyscraper is commensurate with the sudden abundance of steel in the history of our economy, although the first skyscrapers had mostly iron skeletons. The building sometimes considered the first skyscraper, the Home Insurance Company Building in Chicago, built by William Le Baron Jenney in 1885, had cast-iron columns supporting wrought-iron beams on every floor except the first two floors, which were supported entirely by rolled-steel beams. This structure meets another requirement of the skyscraper: it is fire-proofed. Its metal frame is encased in protective brick or clay tiles because both iron and steel soften at high temperatures and lose part of their supportive strength.

Finally, the skyscraper is defined by its foundation. The Egyptian method of spread foot-ings didn't work for skyscrapers since too much weight would bear down on too small an area. Modern builders had to switch to another ancient method, the Roman use of piles, which were driven into the ground all the way to the bedrock.

Despite all these innovations, the skyscraper did not really take off until it could prove itself more welcoming to those who had to use it on a daily basis. Its thousands of tenants

Above: As the sun sinks below the Hudson, the buildings of lower Manhattan glow in the twilight like molten gold against the red sky. To the right is the Verrazano Narrows Bridge, and towering high above it all is the World Trade Center.

needed light, heat, a way to cool off, and a supply of clean air. They also had to communicate easily with each other and with the outside world. For these reasons, the skyscraper cannot easily be defined without reference to other early twentieth-century phenomena, such as the development of electric light and insulated wiring, effective air conditioning and heating, plumbing, and the telephone and the telegraph.

All these hard realities hide behind the impressive aura of the majestic skyscraper. But this is not to say that the skyscraper is a practical architectural concept, in tune with the necessities of the economy or even the convenience of everyday life. On the contrary, skyscrapers have often proven impractical and expensive. It is the exceptional and rare instance when skyscraper design puts a building completely in touch with practical human needs or in harmony with its natural environment. On occasion, when fire has struck or bombs have gone off, such structures have even become death traps. In order to fully grasp the identity and the allure of the skyscraper, we must examine its abstract, aesthetic, and symbolic properties.

In an introductory interview to the book *Skyscrapers,* by Judith Dupré, senior architect Philip Johnson expresses no utopian illusions about the twentieth century's love affair with the skyscraper. The skyscraper, he says, was "an expression, not the result, of economic needs." And that expression, was, to put it baldly, a naked will to power and economic domination, a kind of architectural boasting. Sir Norman Foster, an architect known for his elegant metal-and-glass skyscrapers, also glimpses little practical necessity in the evolution of the skyscraper. All he sees is an ancient and persistent human desire to build toward the sky.

On the other hand, in his introduction to David Bennett's book *Skyscrapers: Form & Function,* Foster admits that his design partner, David Nelson, might strongly disagree with him. Nelson goes so far as to claim that the skyscraper promises a new kind of ecology for an overpopulated world. He envisions a kind of vertical village of the future in which all the needs of a particular population can be served by an immense tower. Given the vast demands of the skyscraper on resources and manpower, this dream will be difficult to realize. And if the dream is realized, it may happen in the densely populated eastern hemisphere, where the skyscraper enjoys its current heyday. Meanwhile, in the West, the skyscraper continues to fascinate and to awe, at least for the time being. It still produces fantasies of grandiosity, expansion, and even fear in those who look up at it or who gaze down from its heights.

■ ■ ■ ■ ■ ■ ■

Opposite: High rises were a solution to congestion but they have proliferated practically everywhere in urban America. To succeed, their goal must be to encourage economic enterprise and accommodate diverse cultural interests. In 1998, the new headquarters of the American Stores Center opened in Salt Lake City, Utah.

Right: The needlelike observation structure near the center of this picture of Calgary, Canada, is known as the Calgary Tower. The building to the right with the illuminated roof is the fifty-two-floor Banker's Hall. Spanning part of its base (but not visible here) is an early 1913 high rise that was left completely intact.

Left: The mile-high city of Denver doesn't have any "mile-high" skyscrapers yet, but clusters of fairly tall high rises now pierce the skyline. The Cash Register Building is prominent in this view from City Park.

Opposite: In Denver, glass curtains create a high-rise trompe l'oeil effect.

Above: In the 1980s, the erection of Manhattan's massive Worldwide Plaza created a stir among its largely low-rent residential neighbors in the adjacent Hell's Kitchen district. Here it is viewed from an apartment fire escape on a foggy night.

Right: The downtown Los Angeles renaissance has ensured the endurance of the skyscraper in the West. Here, the 740-foot (225m) Wells Fargo Towers compete with the 1,018-foot (310m) Library Tower on the right.

Above: The Raffles City Office Tower and the United Overseas Bank Plaza are just a tiny portion of Singapore's impressive skyline. In 1997, Singapore added four identical forty-five-story buildings (not shown here) known as Suntec I, II, III, and IV.

Opposite: The IBM-Quebec Headquarters, completed in 1992, stands as the unchallenged titan of Quebec skyscrapers. Located at 1250 Réné-Levesque in Montreal, its forty-seven stories encompass more than a million square feet (92,903 sq.m).

THE DAWN OF THE SKYSCRAPER

The cow that kicked over Mrs. O'Leary's oil lamp in a Chicago suburb in 1871 started a revolution in office-building construction. The resulting fire destroyed about 18,000 buildings within a two-day period, and the event created an emergency situation that was in part responsible for the development of the skyscraper. Contractors searched for a way to accommodate large numbers of workers in a short amount of time. Partly because downtown Chicago was only a nine-block area hemmed in by the Chicago River and Lake Michigan, the logical solution was to build up rather than out. Meanwhile, the railroad was bringing more and more business to the city. Soon its population would double and real estate prices would soar. Essentially, three

Opposite: The clock tower of Chicago's Wrigley Building. Constructed on a steel frame, this eleven-story Moorish-Renaissance-style structure is a reference to the Giralda Tower in Seville, Spain. The tower features four separate dials, and the dials' hands are made of redwood.

economic conditions converged before the skyscraper really took off in Chicago: expensive land, a lot of capital, and a large labor force. The kind of labor force was important, as well. It had to be white-collar or functionary and require large groups of workers to be in close contact with one another.

The towers built to accommodate big business and a burgeoning population had to be fireproofed, in case of another incendiary disaster. Hand in hand with new inventions, these demands led to an early era in skyscraper building known as the Functional Period. It was during this time that architects and contractors learned how to build tall, safe buildings that could accommodate large groups of tenants and transients. To make the buildings rise higher and higher, the architects rejected the old structures of masonry and experimented with lighter metal skeletons upon which they hung facades of stone and terra-cotta.

EARLY ARCHITECTURAL INNOVATIONS

In 1871, immediately after the great Chicago fire, architect Peter B. Wight read a paper on modern fireproofing to the American Institute of Architects. Realizing that iron loses its strength when it is exposed to high temperatures, he suggested that the undersides of iron beams in public buildings be covered with cement, concrete, or terra-cotta. In the decade that followed, techniques for protecting and strengthening iron and steel proliferated, paving the way for the creation of skeletal structures for tall, strong buildings that were resistant to fire, gravity, and wind. New wind-bracing methods ensured a future for the high rise as well. It was inevitable that a tall building would sway, something that its structure had to withstand safely—without making its occupants seasick or cracking its support structure.

Central heating was yet another advance that benefited the skyscraper. By the 1880s, many buildings had risers and radiator tanks that effectively circulated steam throughout their various units. Ten years later, forced-air ventilation became a staple of the larger buildings. However, office workers in button-down collars or corsets would have to sweat out summers until the years after World War I, when effective air conditioning was in place.

Innovations in plumbing and lighting also coincided with the development of the skyscraper. Plumbing advances were first spurred on by reforms in public health in the 1870s and 1880s. Electric arc lights were already in experimental use in New York City by the end of 1878. By the 1880s the incandescent lamp had replaced the arc light. It would become a common feature in high rises well before the turn of the century.

The vast work forces that filled the skyscrapers needed rapid and effective means of communication. In the new corporations, coworkers might be located ten floors apart from each other. Clients needed to get information and voice their needs rapidly. In the new era of busi-

Opposite: The Fred French Building in Manhattan, photographed here in 1927, the year of its completion. Designed by Sloan & Robertson, this building was the headquarters of the same developer who created Manhattan's innovative residential development Tudor City. The French Building was one of the first skyscrapers to have a flat roof.

NEW YORK TAKES THE LEAD

Chicago may have paved the way for the skyscraper revolution, but New York City was never far behind. After an elite group of architects began changing the skyline of Chicago at the end of the nineteenth century, energetic New York industrialists like the Astors and the Vanderbilts started planning to make the skyscraper into a symbol of their economic might. In 1870 New York could boast little more than six stories to challenge Chicago's skyscraper boom, but by 1895 it had the tallest building in the world, the 306-foot (93m) American Surety Building. Other triumphs followed. The 1903 steel-frame Flatiron Building proved that height could more than make up for width. The triangular structure, only 6 feet (1.8m) wide at its front edge, reached up 285 feet (87m). Its limestone, terra-cotta, and brick were decorated in French Renaissance style, giving the large building a light latticework appearance. In 1908 the 612-foot (187m) Singer Building suddenly rose above all others. Its extravagant brick and terra-cotta surface boasted of the French beaux-arts style. A year later it too was outflanked; this time the giant was the 700-foot (213m) Metropolitan Life Tower, which to many eyes closely resembled the Campanile in Venice's St. Mark's Square.

Left: The MetLife Tower, Manhattan. In 1907, Napoleon LeBrun & Sons were hired to design this tower next to the Metropolitan Life Insurance Building. This classical fifty-story tower is topped by a pyramidal spire, a cupola, and a lantern, with four clocks on each face, each of which is encircled with Italian Renaissance motifs of wreaths and flowers.

Left: Built between 1906 and 1908, the Singer Tower in Manhattan was constructed as a vertical expansion to the Singer Sewing Machine Company. The tower ascended forty-seven stories, topped by an ornate beaux-arts domed roof and lantern. The building was demolished in 1968 and the site was replaced by what is known today as the U.S. Steel Building.

Above: The Flatiron Building under construction in 1902. The radically designed building, named for its triangular shape, was the tallest in the world when it was completed in 1903.

Opposite: The isolated position of Manhattan's Flatiron Building—it's located on a triangular island at the point where two avenues intersect—has permanently offered its tenants some advantages. The space between it and other buildings in the normally choked borough of Manhattan ensures a steady supply of light and air.

ness, profit and speed were more closely intertwined than ever before. That is why the growth of the skyscraper was commensurate with the development of the technologies of the telephone, the typewriter, the telegraph, the mimeograph, and other communication devices.

Although the power-driven elevator is associated with the rise of the skyscraper, it actually predated it. Pulley-and-gear elevators were already in use in English factories by the third decade of the nineteenth century. By 1851, in Yonkers, New York, entrepreneur Elisha Otis had invented the elevator safety brake. Then, in the 1870s, the steam elevator came into use and was soon replaced by the hydraulic elevator, which would just as speedily be put to pasture by the electric elevator.

SKYSCRAPER AESTHETICS

The design of the skyscraper began with some ambiguity. Even if a building didn't need external support, the architect tried to make it look as if it did. Jenney's 256-foot (78m) Home Insurance Company Building in Chicago rose to a height of sixteen stories. Innovative as its metal skeleton was, the building was designed as a visual homage to the past. Its large corner piers and wide cornice existed not for support, but to impart a traditional architectural feeling suggestive of the early Italian Renaissance.

The Home Insurance Building and other early skyscrapers, such as Chicago's 1892 Masonic Temple, which was a tribute to Romanesque style, set the tone for early skyscraper architecture at the end of the nineteenth century. They were economical and well constructed but conservative-looking enough to keep their symbolic links to the past. By the first decade of the twentieth century they would be eclipsed by an eclectic period in skyscraper building. Sober ornamentation would be replaced by showy capitalist icons in the Gothic or Renaissance style. By this time, there was no stopping the proliferation and innovation of the skyscraper in Chicago or New York. It was well on is way to becoming the preeminent symbol of modern urban aspirations.

■ ■ ■ ■ ■ ■ ■

LOUIS SULLIVAN AND THE CHICAGO SCHOOL

Louis Henry Sullivan (1856–1924) was a brilliant innovator of the steel-frame skyscraper. Along with three other Chicago architects, he created the Chicago School, which produced some of the nation's first skyscrapers and had a startling and lasting effect upon twentieth-century urban architecture. Sullivan studied at the Massachusetts Institute of Technology as well as at the Ecole des Beaux-Arts in Paris. He had a knack for combining classical insights with practical considerations, which were finally expressed formally in his 1924 book, *Autobiography of an Idea.* Sullivan's most well-known axiom, "Form follows function," found material expression in two landmark buildings, constructed in partnership with engineer Dankmar Adler: the 1891 Wainwright Building in St. Louis and the 1889 Auditorium Building in Chicago. The Wainwright intrigued the viewer with its strong vertical lines, pulled into prominence by recessed windows. The Auditorium Building heralded the coming of the multiuse building, since it incorporated a hotel, an office building, and a theater with decorative murals overlaid in gold leaf.

Left: The Auditorium Building is especially remarkable for Sullivan's use of the Romanesque revival style, which features a facade of arcades atop a three-story base of granite.

Opposite: In the Wainwright Building the continuous vertical lines of the structural iron skeleton are expressed through the prominent vertical lines along the facade of the building. In this way, Sullivan expressed the character of newly utilized building materials in his design.

Opposite: The Woolworth Building, the grande dame of skyscrapers, takes its skyward aspirations seriously, trying to evoke an idea of weightlessness and airy flight. Although architect Cass Gilbert was a strong believer in Gothic Revival, he was extremely annoyed that the building was dubbed a "cathedral of commerce." This, he claimed, was inaccurate, since his models were all secular, pointing more toward European town halls than churches. Rather than the heavy and mysterious connotations of a church, he wanted to suggest a genteel worldliness.

Right: The Park Row Municipal Building. This New York City legend, built in 1899, comprises an austere upper facade, with brilliant ornamental ledges, and two lavish domes. To this day, the original marble decor and coffered ceiling are still intact.

Below: Chicago's 1894 Reliance Building has never lost its chicness, possibly because of its sheer originality. The preponderance of windows makes it a precursor to the glass curtain-wall buildings that were to come. The lines of its zigzagged bays both fascinate the eye and allow more light for the tenants inside.

Opposite: The John Hancock Center is located on North Michigan Avenue along Chicago's prestigious "Magnificent Mile." The 100-story skyscraper, built in 1969, accommodates offices and luxury residences, shopping, parking, a public observation deck, and a restaurant with a view of the city. The building's tapered form (40,000 square feet [3716sq.m] at the base and 18,000 square feet [1672sq.m] at the summit) allows for both structural stability and spatial efficiency. Seen from this angle, the Hancock Center overshadows the Chicago Water Tower Station (center, foreground), which was completed in 1869 and survived the Chicago fire.

SKYSCRAPER FORM AND STRUCTURE

As in any structure, the stability of the skyscraper begins with its foundation, which in the case of large skyscrapers must be affixed to bedrock. This concern for stability increases with the height of the building, as the question of how to keep such a top-heavy structure on its feet becomes more and more crucial. Vertical gravity load is not the only problem; lateral forces threaten the skyscraper as well in the form of heavy winds and earthquakes.

Wind causes all large high rises to sway, with maximum movement at the very top. Skyscraper structure must strike a balance between rigidity, which could lead to cracking or toppling, and too much flexibility, which would make a skyscraper behave like a palm tree in a tropical windstorm. The optimum wind drift of

Above: New York's Citicorp Building, designed by Stubbins Associates and Emery Roth & Sons, boasts a major innovation in the correction of skyscraper sway. Inside, an enormous concrete block rests on an oiled metal plate. When wind bends the building, the block resists the force, then moves slowly in the same direction as the building.

Above: A closeup of the G.E. Building's ornate, artistic detail.

Right: The Rockefeller Center buildings during a foggy, wet night (circa 1935–1940).

a skyscraper should never exceed $\frac{1}{550}$ of its height. Earthquakes pose a different problem: they threaten to pull apart the skyscraper's supportive skeleton. Wooden structures, due to their inherent flexibility, have always been the least vulnerable to earthquakes, and masonry the most at risk; the steel frame of the skyscraper lies somewhere in between. It takes some ingenuity to ensure that steel frames will withstand a severe earthquake. They must be designed with a quotient of flexibility that will allow them to absorb strong vibrations.

In the later period of skyscrapers, reinforced concrete (concrete hardened within a framework of steel mesh) proved itself resistant to wind and reasonably resistant to tremors, although the cracks that earthquakes caused in it sometimes had to be reinforced with epoxy. This drawback was worth the trouble. Reinforced concrete is not expensive, is adaptable to a wealth of contemporary forms and styles, can be prefabricated in large masses, and perhaps most important, is light in comparison to the load it can handle. Another advantage is that it can be prestressed through a process that involves casting it around stretched steel and then allowing the steel to relax. This technique gives the concrete a better shockproof capacity and an even lighter density. The wall thickness needed to support a steel-frame skyscraper is surprisingly low, sometimes measuring as little as 12 inches (31cm) for the first floor and 4 inches (10cm) for each additional floor.

THE WORLD'S TALLEST BUILDING— FOR A WHILE

In 1974, Chicago's Sears Tower inched its concrete shoulders above the boastful head of New York's World Trade Center. Built in 1972, the World Trade Center's taller twin tower is only 1,368 feet (417m). The Sears Tower is 1,454 feet (443m), not counting its broadcast antennas. At the time, this made it the tallest building in the world.

Rising to 110 floors, the Sears Tower is an example of the innovative bundled-tube structural system, invented by architect Fazlur R. Khan. Bundled tubes give it enough strength to withstand the lateral force of Chicago's heavy winds. The entire structure is composed of modules in the form of nine columnless units that, joined together, create a 225-square-foot (21sq.m) base. Two of these modules end at the fiftieth floor, another two at the sixty-sixth, and three more at the ninetieth, from which extends a two-story tower. The facade of the building is a surface of gleaming black aluminum and bronze-tinted glass. Inside, a system of 104 elevators carries freight as well as the building's daytime population of ten thousand to various locations. Six giant wash robots automatically clean the sides of the building eight times a year. The Sears Tower enjoyed its ascendancy over the vanquished World Trade Center and over every other skyscraper only until 1996, when the newly built Petronas Towers in Kuala Lumpur, Malaysia, outranked it by rising to a height of 1,476 feet (450m).

Right: In shadow, the 61,100 bronze-tinted windows of the Sears Tower fade to black. The looming, oversized structure can seem menacing; only its "Chinese boxes" structure relieves this monotony, ingeniously combining nine separate towers into one. A fault in its design is its inability to buffer Chicago winds effectively. They can feel menacing to visitors to the building, both outside in the plaza below, and in its upper stories.

Above: At this writing, the world's tallest buildings are in Kuala Lumpur, Malaysia. Designed by Cesar Peli, the Petronas Towers function visually like the fortress to an ancient city. Linked by a bridge at the forty-second floor, the two symmetrical towers have a volume several times that of the Empire State Building.

CURTAIN WALLS AND SKYSCRAPER SKELETONS

Lightness and strength are the twin requirements of the skyscraper wall. Unlike brick walls, which are constructed from the ground up, the walls of a skyscraper are hung like curtains from the skeleton, and they need the comparative lightness of curtains if they are not to bring their scaffolding down with them. The relatively light load delegated to them means that they can be dedicated to other functions. This is where the decorative aspects of the skyscraper's facade come into play, as evidenced by the intricate carvings and recessed patterns on the sky-scrapers of the past. Architects can also exploit the curtain wall by increasing the size and number of windows, to the extent that some contemporary buildings have become towers mostly of glass.

The nature of the skyscraper skeleton depends in part upon the demands of its height. The earliest skyscrapers had rigid metal frames. Skyscrapers under 300 feet (92m) are still built with rigid frames in steel and concrete. The joints between the beams are welded together or affixed with concrete. An even stronger structure is achieved by constructing a steel vertical truss inside a rigid frame or adding a concrete shear wall to provide more rigidity. Buildings of this type can reach a height of 500 feet (152m). Next comes the framed-tube structure, composed of steel and concrete, which transfers part of the building's load to a series of columns around the building's perimeter. Such a structure can reach heights of 1,000 feet (305m) and still withstand lateral wind forces. The trussed-tube structure has interior rather than exterior columns, with diagonal bracing all around the perimeter of the skyscraper. It can support heights of up to 1,200 feet (366m). Finally, there is the bundled tube, made up of a collection of framed tubes joined together by reinforcements, which have allowed the skyscraper to reach heights nearing 1,500 feet (457m).

■ ■ ■ ■ ■ ■ ■

Above: The complicated stacked structure of the Fred French Building in New York gave the idea of the setback a new and ingenious aestheticism. The building appears to offer to the onlooker a series of jeweled and studded boxes.

Left: Horizontal bands of glass and red granite define this oval tower in Manhattan, completed in 1986. Designed by Philip Johnson, it was quickly dubbed the Lipstick Building for its resemblance to the telescoping shaft of a tube of lipstick. Johnson assiduously avoided superfluous garnishes, opting instead for an uninterrupted though highly eccentric shape.

Above: Red brick and cast iron trimmed with terra-cotta distinguish the Potter Building, an early high rise designed by architect Norris G. Starkweather. Built between 1883 and 1886, it rose on Manhattan's Park Row to a then breathtaking height of eleven stories, with two more stories below ground. The thick walls—necessary before the steel skeleton was perfected—and the heavy interior support columns infringe on the available space. Even so, there is room for more than two hundred offices.

Above: The Flatiron Building was among the first steel-cage structures to be erected in Manhattan. Part Gothic and part Renaissance in style, it is divided into vertical sections like a classical column or a decorated layer cake.

Opposite: The sunburst structures at the top of the Chrysler Building are covered with a combination of chrome and nickel, known as Nirosta metal. The windows are triangular, further contributing to the sunburst motif. Completed in 1930, the Chrysler Building was one of the last flamboyant gestures of its era; structures that followed it were much less extravagant.

Left: The twin towers of the World Trade Center in lower Manhattan. Their design, by the American architect Yimoru Yamasaki, has been criticized for its unforgiving severity. The face of the towers is a shiny, metallic shell composed of narrow channels.

Above: The World Trade Center under construction in the early 1970s. When the towers were built they were the best-known example of the framed tube structure.

Left: The Empire State Building is seen here under construction in 1930. As many as 3,400 workers toiled against gravity to construct this edifice, for combined labor amounting to approximately seven million hours. The building was finished in one year and forty-five days, which included Sundays and holidays. When it was finished, about five thousand people crowded together to watch Alfred E. Smith cement a giant cornerstone with a silver trowel.

Opposite: Perhaps nowhere is the full flowering of the Gothic Revival
so evident as in Chicago's 1925 Tribune Tower, designed by Raymond
Hood and John Mead Howells. References to the cathedral of Rouen
in France are intentional. The crown, shown here, is an airy network of
flying buttresses and open tracery. Louis Sullivan later criticized this
building as unimaginative, and in many ways it marked the beginning
of the end of the Gothic Revival. Nevertheless, the building continues
to occupy an important place in the history of the skyscraper.

Above: Chicago's Amoco Building, completed in 1974, seems out of
place when seen from this isolating perspective. It has been the target
of resentment from a number of Chicagoans, who criticize it for a lack
of corner offices and because its original marble cladding was replaced
by granite. Its height dwarfs the more fanciful Two Prudential Plaza
(1990) to the left.

Above and left: Officially known as Marina Towers, these two towers on a small marina near the Chicago River are irreverently referred to as "the corn cobs" by some locals because of their shape and their rows of kernellike balconies. Each has sixteen stories of offices and forty-one stories of apartments.

Below: The Pittsburgh Plate Glass Building Tower is glazed with 19,750 pieces of glass. After more than sixty years in which skyscraper architects had eschewed the Gothic Revival aesthetic for high rises, the team of John Burgee Architects with Philip Johnson returned to it with this design in the early 1980s, giving a contemporary, mirror-palace slant to the old tradition.

Opposite: I.M. Pei & Partners designed Boston's John Hancock Tower, which overlooks Copley Square. Despite the stark appearance of the sixty-story structure, its reflective blue glass and rhomboid shape gestured away from the International Style. Before completion in 1976, its windows began to fall out; more than 10,000 panes had to be replaced. The building has been criticized on aesthetic grounds for its jarring juxtaposition with historical Boston, an accent of which appears here in the lamp sconces jutting from the Boston Public Library.

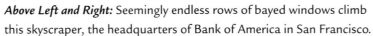
Above Left and Right: Seemingly endless rows of bayed windows climb this skyscraper, the headquarters of Bank of America in San Francisco.

Opposite: Designed by Henry N. Cobb working with I.M. Pei & Partners, the First Interstate Bank Tower in Dallas was built in 1986. In its time the glass curtain-wall was the largest in existence, with a total area of more than 500,000 square feet (46,452sq.m). The building has a square base; it then divides into a complex interlocking of cubes, rhomboids, and other solids.

Above: This building is the second of three Federal Reserve buildings in Minneapolis, Minnesota. This structure is actually supported like a bridge by two end pillars and was designed to hold additional stories if ever needed.

Opposite: Toronto's Nathan Phillips Square, designed by Finnish architect Viljo Revell, opened in 1965. The two curved towers shielding it, behind the overturned saucer structure, are the New City Hall. The spectacular success of this structure resides primarily in the generous allocation of public space around it. There are clear views from all the windows in both towers of the square, which offers a skating rink in winter and a reflecting pool in the summer.

Above: The Woolworth Building proved a formidable project from the very beginning. Sixty-nine caissons were sunk into the bedrock, some supported by plate girders. The two lowest floors were constructed with reinforced concrete, and hollow tile was used for the upper floors. The ornamentation of the building was complex and expensive, involving veined marble from Skyros and bronze trimming. Here, the tip of the Woolworth protrudes majestically through the clouds.

Opposite: The 1929 Chanin Building, seen in detail here, was once the tallest building in midtown Manhattan. In rebellion against the Gothic style of ornamentation typified by the Woolworth Building, this building favored bold Art Deco ornamentation accomplished by ornate bas-reliefs.

SKYSCRAPER FUNCTION

Skyscrapers have always forced a compromise between aesthetic considerations and practical functions. Ambivalence about the skyscraper as symbol versus the skyscraper as practical edifice was present as early as the construction of New York's sumptuous Woolworth Building (1910–13). In order to provide a return on the lavish investment that went into this building, its creators realized that the proportion of office space to elevator space was crucial, and that windows had to be installed in such a way that no office would be left without light. The fact that this impressive monument to big business had to accommodate living humans just as much as it had to serve as an urban icon led to a host of practical concessions. Enormous expense went into

Opposite: After the building of the United Nations Plaza Hotel in 1976, two taller structures created by Kevin Roche, John Dinkeloo and Associates were added. These towers, with their smooth skin of gleaming blue-green glass, are a late tribute to the International style. Plans for a much more extensive complex were canceled during the 1970s because of a downslide in the real estate market.

Above: Inside the BCE Place arcade, Toronto, Ontario. BCE Place includes this fanciful, light-infused galleria designed by Bredman & Hamann. Its sweeping, curved metal beams, which support a glass roof, are meant to symbolize the maple trees of Canada. Built into one wall of the mezzanine is the facade of an old bank.

making the system of twenty-six elevators as safe and as fast as possible. When the building opened, the elevators could travel between 600 and 700 feet (183–213m) a minute. The high-cost water supply system was partitioned into seven different functions, which included service to toilets, fire protection outlets, and a basement swimming pool. In the end, the functional aspects of the Woolworth Building were as impressive and innovative as its appearance. It was, in a way, a precursor of skyscrapers that followed, all of which had to come face to face with the often costly needs of their human tenants and visitors.

Until after World War II, many skyscrapers were designed so that each successive module was farther and farther recessed from the street. The buildings thus rose in stepwise fashion, becoming thinner as they got taller. These buildings showed a full consciousness of the fact that part of the advantage of the high rise is the fact that it offers occupants an unobstructed bird's-nest access to light and fresh air. But this luxury meant that there was less and less floor space to rent the higher the building became. Following World War II, the skyscraper rejected these concessions. The progressively stepped skyscraper gave way to a more boxlike form, pro-

moted by the International Style. By the late 1970s, however, there were complaints about the stark inhumanity of such skyscrapers. Zoning laws began forcing builders to plan parks and shopping areas around the base of any high rise above a certain number of stories. Skyscrapers were pressured to become real—rather than symbolic—benefactors of the community. In the eighties, mini-malls, entertainment complexes, and gymnasiums became required components of the skyscraper. This was hardly a new concept. A skyscraper "village" called Rockefeller Center, which had ample space for pedestrians and shops, had pioneered such an approach more than fifty years before.

Above: Several skyscrapers steal the show in the Dallas skyline. On the left is the fifty-story Reunion Tower, topped by an observation sphere that offers a view of the whole city.

THE SKYSCRAPER'S SECRET LIFE

To the casual observer, the twentieth century's behemoth skyscrapers, like the Sears Tower and the World Trade Center, seem impervious and self-sufficient, blankly out of touch with human functions. In reality, these buildings are hugely dependent upon regular maintenance,

MAINTAINING THE
EMPIRE STATE BUILDING

Keeping the 1,454-foot (443m), 365,000-ton Empire State Building shipshape is no easy task. Its 6,500 windows require regular washes to remove the grime that settles out of Manhattan's polluted air. All seventy-three of its elevators, which together cover hundreds of miles daily at breathtaking speeds, need frequent testing and lightning-quick repairs. The 50 miles (80km) of radiator pipes in the building must be inspected and protected from rust and clogging. More than a thousand miles (1,600km) of telephone cable keep telephone lines bristling with activity. These, too, must be checked and repaired. Each month, about 100 tons (90t) of trash are removed from the Empire State Building. All of this is accomplished by a mere 250 people, which includes a maintenance staff of about 150.

Above: This long channel runs to the top of the Empire State Building, flanked by two rectangular columns that undergo a series of setbacks. The materials are limestone and stainless steel, a cost-saving measure of the time.

much of it designed to make their occupants as comfortable and safe as possible. Long after the business tenants have left the buildings or the residential tenants have gone to bed, the various staffs needed to maintain a large high rise begin their work. There is not a morning when trucks do not pull up to unload their many provisions at the service entrance of the big skyscrapers in the wan light of dawn. Frozen and fresh food for the cafeterias and restaurants, thousands of pieces of daily mail, paper goods for the hundreds of washrooms, countless light bulbs, and gallons of cleaning supplies are all part of the regular caravan into the building.

But what comes in is no more mind-boggling than what goes out. Every day more than a ton of trash is removed from the tallest skyscrapers. Thousands of gallons of waste water leave by the labyrinthine plumbing system. Electricity is gulped up by office complexes and condominiums. This is the skyscraper's largest expense, generated by huge substations through thousands of miles of electrical cable. Part of this power goes to the skyscraper's chillers, each of which can weigh several tons. These chillers pump air through cooled water, and then channel it to each floor.

At night, when the building is nearly empty, daily maintenance begins. The refuse-collection crew starts its long journey. A massive team of cleaners invades the empty offices. Maintenance of the electrical wiring, plumbing, elevators, windows, and air ducts starts another round in an endless cycle of improvements. Meanwhile, in the building command center, a team may keep careful watch on a series of video monitors that show what is happening in every corner of the vast space. Another set of screens is connected to computers, which constantly survey the several pieces of heavy machinery needed to run the building.

In recent years, more and more large skyscrapers have been designed to accommodate residential tenants. The John Hancock Center in Chicago has hundreds of office tenants, several stores, a hotel, and a section of condominiums, making it the tallest multiuse building in the world. Its seven hundred or so condominium owners are served by their own post office, supermarket, and garbage-collection system. But they are isolated from the street, often dependent on their doorkeepers to find out about events and weather conditions on the ground.

■ ■ ■ ■ ■ ■ ■

Above: Few new visitors to New York City fail to notice the angled roof of the Citicorp Center. The aluminum covered roof faces south and slopes at a 45° angle.

Right: In the late 1980s, Eighth Avenue in midtown Manhattan was mostly an unsavory extension of prerenovated Times Square, but that didn't stop the construction of the massive Worldwide Plaza. This condominium and office complex now fills an entire block between Eighth and Ninth Avenues and 49th and 50th Streets. The enclosed ground-floor arcade is circular, encouraging a profusion of specialty shops. The building has a pink facade and a large pyramidal roof.

Above and Right: Lake Point Tower in Chicago looms above a Ferris wheel. Built in 1968, this seventy-story condominium, based partly on a sketch made by Mies van der Rohe in 1921, was designed by two students, John Heinrich and George Schipporeit. The building has three wings, each forming a 120-degree angle, affording an unencumbered view to all tenants.

Right: Sunset on the Sears Tower. Subdued as this giant may seem at dusk, it is a twenty-four-hour hive of industry and activity. Aside from the crew of night maintenance workers, there is an investment firm on the twenty-third floor that operates twenty-four hours a day. A single restaurant serves sandwiches to the graveyard shift halfway through the night. Some boutiques and souvenir shops on the lower level are open until 11 P.M.

Right: Some of the tallest skyscrapers in the Chicago skyline seem about to pierce the heavy clouds.

Above: It's hard to decide which is more entrancing—the evening light show of the romantic Buckingham Fountain in Chicago's Grant Park at the lake front, or the dazzling array of skyscrapers that forms a backdrop to it. Slightly to the left is the Amoco Building, looking like a detached cathedral spire.

Below: Built in 1985, International Place in Boston was designed by architect Philip Johnson.

Above: Designed by John Portman in 1978, the Westin Bonaventure Hotel and Suites is one of the most photographed skyscrapers in Los Angeles. Its six-level atrium lobby contains more than thirty restaurants and shops. Five glass-curtained cylindrical towers rise from a single concrete base. Like the Peachtree Hotel, also designed by Portman in the 1970s, this building represents the optimistic apotheosis of the decade's urbanism.

Above: Despite its relative diminutiveness, the Gooderham Building (also known as the Flatiron) in downtown Toronto is still a local landmark. Designed in 1892 by David Roberts, it could not contrast any more strongly with the contemporary BCE Place rearing up behind it. BCE Place was designed in the 1990s by architects Skidmore, Owings and Merrill.

THE HEYDAY OF THE SKYSCRAPER

The skyscraper boom began in the nineteenth century as a hopeful but cautious response to a burgeoning economy and its new emphasis on urban life. In the first fifteen years of the twentieth century, architects indulged themselves in bolder and bolder experiments. Since the skyscraper was a new form, several stylistic directions were open to it. The details of its facade could recall classicism or project science-fiction futurism; its height and stunningly modern accommodations could transport both onlookers and occupants into a strictly modernist world. By the 1920s, this eclecticism and modernity were becoming exaggerated. The skyscraper flowered into a dominant, flamboyant urban phenomenon. The competition to build taller and taller

Opposite: Built cheaply during the Great Depression, the Empire State Building holds locals and visitors in neck-craning awe to this day. In July 1945, the building underwent the ultimate test of its strength and stability when it survived the head-on collision of a B-25 bomber that caused a gaping hole in its seventy-ninth floor.

Right: The design of the Tribune Tower in Chicago by architects Raymond M. Hood and John Mead Howells inspired the *Chicago Tribune* to hold a "most beautiful building in the world" contest in 1922. The Tribune Tower is studded with stones from famous sites all over the world.

buildings found full force during these years. The skyscraper really became a corporate icon as large companies exploited it to lend power and status to their images.

STYLE DEVELOPMENTS

If the 1913 Woolworth Building, with its Gothic tower and U-shaped base, dominates the eclectic period of the skyscraper, the 1930 Chrysler Building is at the pinnacle of the next wave, which became known as Art Deco. Designed by William Van Alen, it pierced the Manhattan skyline with its eerie eccentricity, produced by a series of silver scalloped sunbursts ending in a needle. Geometrical symmetry dominated its facade, and in reference to its owner, Walter P. Chrysler, radiator caps portraying Mercury were placed at various points along the building.

Other New York buildings from this period, such as the 1926 Barclay-Vesey Building, the home of the New York Telephone Company, banned all references to historical style from their facades in the name of modernity. Stressing verticality, their modules sprouted into multiple setbacks like spiky juggernauts. Still others reached for the exotic or boldly experimented with color. The McGraw-Hill Building, on 42nd Street, was paneled in grayish-aqua and trimmed with gold. The 450 Sutter Building, in San Francisco, exploited the aesthetic of the Mayan pyramid. The Miller, Pflueger, & Cantin Building, also in San Francisco, made use of Chinese motifs.

The stock market crash of 1929, followed by World War II, temporarily squelched the sky-scraper revolution. It also forced architects and builders to take stock of the International Style, which had been formulated in Europe before the war. For the first time, function and cost-effectiveness became the preeminent values in the building of high rises. Despite the aus-tere and totalitarian look of many of these plain, geometric monoliths, their inspiration came from social, communal values, an attempt to transform the elements of industrialism into a humanist aesthetic. Conveniently, postwar America provided the perfect stage for this new pared-down approach. Urban real estate had become excessively expensive and handmade dec-orative crafts were a dying art. The generic glass box began to dominate skyscraper architec-ture, with only a few examples, like Mies van der Rohe's Seagram Building, distinguishing themselves from the common variety.

Over the next two decades, the values of the International Style seemed shorn of their ini-tial idealism. Nevertheless, the rectangular monoliths they inspired continued to proliferate. Now the competition for height was in deadly earnest. Buildings like New York's One World Trade Center (1972; 1,368 feet/417m) and Chicago's Amoco Building (1973; 1,136 feet/346m) and Sears Tower (1974; 1,454 feet/443m) raced toward world records, only to fall behind just a few years later. It wasn't until the late seventies that public opinion and ecological pressures forced a reassessment of this trend. By the 1980s a new direction had become apparent. Called postmodernism by some, it featured a nostalgic but highly eclectic return to classical orna-mentation as well as a new regard for ecological concerns. The cooler-controlled building with its sealed windows gave way in some cases to tinted glass walls that reduced the heat factor of the sun. Malls, parks, and playgrounds created "breathing space" around the new high rises.

■ ■ ■ ■ ■ ■ ■

Above: In 1950, the Empire State Building's status as the highest structure in the world seemed assured. A 222-foot (381m) television antenna added that year increased its height even further. However, by 1954, the building had already lost the race for height. In 1985, partly for technological reasons but also because the race for height no longer mattered, the old antenna was replaced by this shorter one.

MIES VAN DER ROHE
(1886–1969)

German-born Ludwig Mies van der Rohe was the master of the International Style. His place in the modernist revolution was already assured at the age of twenty-one, when he became involved with a group of German artists and craftsmen who were developing an aesthetic that celebrated machine-made things. This led to Mies's interest in pure function. He envisioned buildings whose primary visual character was influenced by their actual structural demands, rather than by any decorative dramatization.

In 1929, Mies designed the German Pavilion for the International Exposition at Barcelona. It featured a series of spacious, nearly empty rooms under a thin roof supported by steel columns. Its walls were made of onyx, marble, and frosted glass.

After moving to the United States in 1937, Mies became director of the School of Architecture at Chicago's Armour Institute. After World War II, he designed his most famous steel-skeleton skyscrapers, rectangular monoliths with no ornamentation and with glass-curtain walls. Most famous of these is the Seagram Building in New York, which Mies designed in 1956 with Philip Johnson.

In the last decade of his life, Mies designed several other noteworthy skyscrapers, including the One Charles Center office building in Baltimore. His work influenced a whole generation of architects working in America, but less then ten years after his death, his spare geometric aesthetic came under attack, leading to the dominance of the postmodern style.

Right: Perhaps the most triumphantly naked expression of the steel frame is the Seagram Building, with its glass curtain-wall. Though it rises to a height of thirty-eight stories, its placement above a spacious, glass-enclosed lobby keeps it from dominating public space, as was to happen later when the unadorned high rise became a cliché in Manhattan.

Right: The MetLife Building (formerly known as the Pan Am Building) owes its octagonal design to the architects Walter Gropius and Pietro Belluschi. At the time of the building's erection in 1963, its intrusive concrete facade outraged some local preservationists who felt that it had dwarfed the landscape of Park Avenue and threatened Grand Central Station, whose facade has been practically incorporated by this building.

Above: The Lever Building, Manhattan, built by Skidmore, Owings & Merrill with Gordon Bunshaft. This building pioneered skyscraper construction by replacing old style use of masonry walls with the more modern use of glass curtains and stainless steel sheathing. On the street level there is a beautiful garden atrium.

Above: The Graybar Building, at the corner of Lexington Avenue and 42nd Street in Manhattan, was built of steel and completed in 1927.

Opposite: At dusk the Chrysler Building is unmistakably delineated from some of its more recent skyscraper neighbors. Believe it or not, this highly original structure went through a couple decades of neglect, especially in the 1970s, before it underwent a major restoration in the early 1980s.

Above: A vertical view of details of the Chanin Building with the Chrysler Building shooting skyward on the left. In the 1930s, innovative photographers like Berenice Abbot would use these proximities to capture breathtaking images of the skyscraper. From the Chanin building, photographers had a bird's-eye view of the Chrysler building. And from the top of the Chrysler Building, they could photograph the decorative crown of the Chanin Building.

Opposite: Originally designed as an evocation of the Campanile in Venice's Piazza San Marco, the 700-foot (213m) marble Metropolitan Life Insurance Tower, designed by Napoleon LeBrun & Sons, emphatically changed the landscape of what was at the time considered uptown Manhattan. When the tower was refaced with limestone in 1960, most of the original ornaments were removed, but the wreaths and flowers around the clock faces survived.

Right: This seventy-one-story, 927-foot (283m) building at 40 Wall Street, Manhattan, was built in 1930 by the Bank of Manhattan Company. It was finished off with a pyramidal top and lantern. At the time of construction, it was competing with the Chrysler Building, also in the process of construction, for the world's tallest, and perhaps would have won if the architects of the Chrysler building hadn't snuck a fully assembled spire onto the top of their building shortly after 40 Wall Street was completed.

Left: The Woolworth Building is still regal after all these years. Crowned by its easily identifiable pinnacle, this structure accomplishes the seemingly impossible: it soars to a height of 792 highly functional feet (241m) without losing a shred of its humanity. Its references to Gothic architecture may once have inspired cynical jokes about "cathedrals of commerce," but its stately elegance has made it an enduring New York City landmark.

Opposite: Separated by sixty years of architectural innovation, both of these Manhattan buildings are still the focus of unending interest in style and function. Though they were dedicated to the same profit-making purposes, the difference in their appearance shows how radically architectural values changed in the interim. The World Trade Center (left) is severe and monolithic, unforgivingly stolid against the Manhattan night sky. The Woolworth Building's Neo-Gothic presence (right) is an eye-catcher, with its gorgeously lit Gothic top.

Left: Like gates to some vertical city of the future, the unadorned towers of the World Trade Center stand guard to Manhattan's rich and varied architectural past.

Above: Designed in 1915 by Peabody and Sterns, the Custom House Tower in Boston (seen here in detail) is nearly overburdened with classical ornamentation. The thirty-story structure is known as the Clock Tower because of its ornate clock (top, left). At almost five hundred feet (152m) high, it was Boston's first very tall building.

Opposite: The Custom House Tower, Boston, Massachusetts, photographed in 1920 from the end of Commercial Street.

Above: In the 1950s, Frank Lloyd Wright designed his only skyscraper. This nineteen-story glass and copper skyscraper for H. C. Price of Price Pipeline is located in Bartlesville, Oklahoma. It was meant to accommodate both office tenants and apartment dwellers. The design is based on a diamond pattern of thirty– and sixty-degree angles.

Above: Chicago's famed Wrigley Building. Built in 1921 to honor the widespread popularity of William Wrigley's chewing gum, this building has a facade composed of six shades of glazed terra-cotta, ranging from cream to bluish gray. Even today, it is cleaned periodically by hand.

CHAPTER FIVE

POSTMODERNISM AND BEYOND

By the late 1970s it had become clear that architects were rejecting the legacy of the International Style. But in rebelling against this modernist architecture they suddenly found themselves on shaky ground: how could a style be "new" if it wasn't dependent upon the old modernist utopian myths of progress and individual vision? Their solution to this dilemma cannot be termed a revolution in architecture, but it represents a new freedom of approach to structure and ornamentation.

In the 1980s, these architects reclaimed older styles of ornamentation, using them not as authoritarian models but as a palette, whose "colors" they mixed in ways that would have been considered irreverent in the past. Lying somewhere between a

Opposite: This thirty-six-story office tower at 333 Wacker Drive in Chicago just fits its triangular site along the Chicago River. The side facing the river is a vast curtain-wall of green glass. The base is gray granite striped with green marble. The first floor is positioned just above the elevated train.

new traditionalism and the rebellious experimentations of modernism, postmodernism has altered the urban face of America with skyscrapers like Philip Johnson and John Henry Burgee's AT&T Building, which boasts a Chippendale skyline. Other postmodern architects have been promoting more obvious revivalist values. Their buildings are facsimiles of the Art Deco period, but it is as if they had put lighthearted quotation marks around the style. An example is Helmet Jan's 1982 Bank of the Southwest, which resembles an Art Deco glass skyscraper.

Despite this new eclecticism and reclamation of the past, the future of the skyscraper in the West for the next century remains uncertain. As mentioned before, the emphasis on high rises has moved to the East and especially the Pacific Rim, where height and an aggressive corporate dominance of the landscape continue to be valued. Whether the dream of skyscraper as "vertical village" will ever be realized in either hemisphere remains to be seen. All sorts of proposals for a new kind of high rise are being offered by younger architects, from buildings that run on solar power and recycle wastes to those whose windows can actually be opened and those that have living foliage integrated into their structure and ornamentation. But no one can predict with real certainty whether the skyscraper will continue to survive, not only as the preeminent urban structure, but as an ideal.

■ ■ ■ ■ ■ ■

Left: The ever-growing skyscraper increased the space for light and air by use of setbacks. With the Transamerica Pyramid of San Francisco, completed in 1972, the idea has been taken to its logical conclusion, resulting in two constant oblique lines forming a skinny pyramid. The building was designed by Chicago-trained architect William Pereira.

Opposite: Illuminated skyscrapers turn Hong Kong into a geometric fantasy-scape after dark. In the center is the Bank of China, designed by I.M. Pei. With four columns rising from a granite base, its glass tower exudes an airiness and delicacy that have earned it a reputation as one of the most elegant skyscrapers in the world.

Right: Central Tower, Hong Kong, China. By its completion in 1992, it was the tallest building in Asia, standing 1,227 feet (374m) and seventy-eight stories high. However, the 1998 construction of the Jin Mao Tower in Shanghai surpassed the height of Central Tower, rising an impressive 1,379 feet (421m) and eighty-eight stories into the air. The new millenium can expect other colossal architectural feats in China with the construction of the International Finance Centre in Hong Kong (eighty-eight stories; projected completion, 2003), the Shanghai World Financial Center (ninety-four stories; projected completion, 2001), and the Post and Telecommunications Building (sixty-three stories; projected completion, 2000).

Above: Perspective diminishes the Petronas Towers in Kuala Lumpur, Malaysia, which are just visible through the smog at dawn. From a great distance, they look like the spires of a Gothic cathedral. Closer up, they take on an Eastern appearance, in a whirl of complicated geometric elements, which are a reference to Islamic beliefs about the mysterious symmetries of the universe.

Above: The glass curtain-walls of a neighboring building create a funhouse image of Manhattan's Lipstick Building, revealing the fractured face of postmodernism.

Left: Internationalism's hold on skyscraper design was broken in 1984 with the completion of this first masterpiece of postmodern design, the Sony Building (formerly the AT&T Building) in Manhattan. The brainchild of Philip Johnson, it immediately became controversial. At the top of its granite facade, the circular cleft in its pediment associates it with the design of Chippendale furniture. A series of arches at street level creates a gallery sixty-five feet (20m) high.

Opposite: Completed in 1983, the 738-foot (225m) First Union Financial Center in downtown Miami is fifty-five stories high, making it the tallest building in Florida. One of several sophisticated postmodern skyscrapers built in the area during the real estate boom of the eighties, it was resold for $208 million in 1997.

Above: Rialto Tower, Melbourne, Australia. These twin towers are encased by 193,749 square feet (17,800sq.m) of glass that reflects the colors of the sky. Rialto Tower is the tallest building in the southern hemisphere at 832 feet (253m) and the seventh tallest reinforced concrete building in the world.

Above: Boldly silhouetted against a nearly naked skyline, the seventy-story Peachtree Plaza Hotel, built in 1976, seemed to rule downtown Atlanta until other skyscrapers appeared near it. This simple column of reflecting glass affords maximum space and breathtaking views to the higher of the thousand or so guest rooms. The hotel originally featured a lake, waterfalls, hanging terraces, and a menagerie of animals at the lobby level, but some of these features were lost when the building was renovated in 1987.

Above: The charming Seattle skyline is punctuated by the sun-reflecting Two Union Square building (center), completed in 1989, which rises fifty-six stories and 741 feet (226m), making it Seattle's second tallest building. In the distance (left) is the Columbia Seafirst Center, Seattle's tallest building at seventy-six stories and 942 feet (287m).

Below: The Scotia Bank Tower (built between 1974 and 1977) is one of the tallest buildings in the city of Vancouver. It is several dozen feet higher than the usual city limit of 400 feet (122m). A smaller, older building was torn down to make room for a retail module next to it.

Opposite: Built in 1988 by Kohn Pedersen Fox Associates, the fifty-five-floor Washington Mutual Tower is the third tallest building in Seattle. A high ledge on its east face provided shelter for the city's very first downtown family of peregrines.

Left: Chicago's Amoco Building has an unrelenting vertical severity. At eighty stories and 1,136 feet (346m) high, it is the second tallest building in the city. Its steel structure is hung with gray granite from Mount Airy. The postmodern shadow against it is cast by Two Prudential Plaza.

Opposite: At 1,018 feet (310m) high, the Library Tower (right) in downtown Los Angeles ranks as one of the tallest buildings in the West. Designed by I.M. Pei & Partners between 1988 and 1990, the circular granite and glass tower decreases in diameter by a series of complicated setbacks as it rises.

SKYSCRAPERS OF THE FUTURE

As the eclecticism and revivalist tendencies of the Postmodern period fade into the past, the temptation to speculate about the future of the skyscraper, especially given the benefits of modern technology, is irresistaible. Remarkable technological developments have enabled architects to glimpse the future as never before, through high-tech models and computer-generated renderings of proposed buildings. At this writing, the Taichung Tower II and the Shanghai World Financial Center (shown below), both designed by Kohn Pedersen Fox Associates of New York, are under construction and scheduled for completion during the first decade of the twenty-first century. Such vivid renderings of these structures make it possible to visualize skyscrapers in situ years in advance of their completion. Even more extraordinary than these images are the structures themselves and the amazing materials and techniques that will one day make them a reality. The engineering and construction of such colossal towers are architectural feats of the highest order.

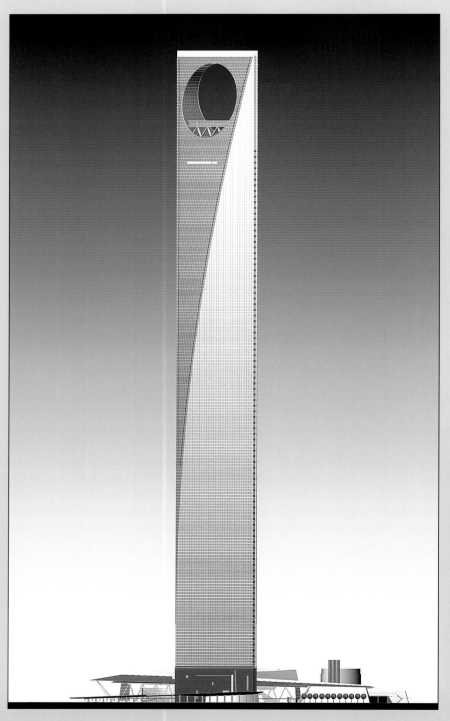

Left: A computerized rendering of the proposed Shanghai World Financial Center, Shanghai, China. When completed, this skyscraper—at 1,509 feet (460m) and ninety-five stories—will be among the tallest in the world. The building will stand on a site in the Lujiazui Financial and Trade district of Pudong, China's newly designated hub of international banking and trading. It will house a five-star hotel, retail and office space, and an observation deck at the top level. Two primary forms are used in the design of this skyscraper: a square prism and a cylinder. The two intersect and result in a unique sculptural form. A "moon gate" is carved through the upper portion of the tower to relieve wind pressure at the top.

Left: A model of the proposed Taichung Tower II in Taichung, Taiwan. At forty-seven stories this building will house a hotel and offices when it is completed. This futuristic structure, which curves on two sides, is highly sculptural in form. While developing the design for the tower, the architects realized that the plan resembled the form of a fish. Researching the origins of Chinese symbolism they discovered to their delight that a fish facing East is interpreted in Taiwan as good fortune.

Bennet, David. *Skyscrapers: Form & Function*. New York: Simon & Schuster, 1995.

Dupré, Judith. *Skyscrapers*. New York: Black Dog & Leventhal Publishers, 1996.

Landau, Sarah Bradford, and Condit, Carl W. *Rise of the New York Skyscraper, 1865–1913*. New Haven: Yale University Press, 1996.

Lewis, Hilary, and John O'Connor. *Philip Johnson: The Architect in His Own Words*. New York: Rizzoli, 1994.

Scuri, Piera. *Late-Twentieth-Century Skyscrapers*. New York: Van Nostrand Reinhold, 1990.

Tauranac, John. *The Empire State Building: The Making of a Landmark*. New York: Scribner, 1995.

Twombly, Robert. *Power and Style: A Critique of Twentieth-Century Architecture in the United States*. New York: Hill and Wang, 1995.

Sabbagh, Karl. *Skyscraper: The Making of a Building*. New York: Penguin, 1990.

Wiseman, Carter. *The Architecture of I.M. Pei*. London: Thames & Hudson, 1990.

INDEX